The Lost Smile

Christian Holzmann

HELBLING LANGUAGES
www.helblinglanguages.com

The Lost Smile
by Christian Holzmann
© HELBLING LANGUAGES 2007

First published 2007

ISBN 978-3-85272-029-6

The publishers would like to thank the following for their kind permission to reproduce the following photographs and other copyright material: Alamy p28 (Hagrid), p29 (claustrophobia); Corbis p28 (Dobby); ©iStockphoto.com /weareadventurers p29; Shutterstock Alexander Sysoev, Anna Chelnokova, vadim kozlovsky James M Phelps Jr, Robynrg p29.

Series editor Maria Cleary
Activities by Elspeth Rawstron
Illustrated by Stefano Misesti
Design and layout by Pixarte
Printed by Athesia

About this Book

For the Student

🎧 Listen to all of the story and do some activities on your Audio CD

💬 Talk about the story

tune° When you see the green dot you can check the word in the glossary

For the Teacher

Go to our Readers Resource site for information on using readers and downloadable Resource Sheets, photocopiable Worksheets, Answer Keys and Tapescripts.

Plus the full version of the story on MP3.
www.helblinglanguages.com/readers

For lots of great ideas on using Graded Readers consult Reading Matters, the Teacher's Guide to using Helbling Readers.

Level 3 Structures

Present continuous for future	Cardinal / ordinal numbers
Present perfect	One / ones
Present perfect versus past simple	Reflexive pronouns
Should / shouldn't (advice and obligation)	Indefinite pronouns
Must / should	
Need to / have to	Too plus adjective
Will	Not plus adjective plus enough
	Relative pronouns who, which and that
Ever / never	Prepositions of time, place and movement
Would like	
So do I / neither do I	
Question tags	

Structures from lower levels are also included

Contents

Before Reading

1 Look at the pictures in the book. What kind of story is it?

a) ☐ fantasy   **c)** ☐ romance

b) ☐ horror   **d)** ☐ science fiction

2 Match the pictures with the words.

a) witch   **b)** wizard   **c)** goblin   **d)** dwarf   **e)** vampire   **f)** giant

☐   ☐   ☐

 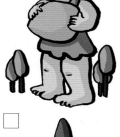 

☐   ☐   ☐

**3 Can you see any of these characters in this book?
Look at the pictures.**

4 In pairs, ask and answer the questions.

Do you like fantasy books?
What is your favourite fantasy book?
Who is you favourite fantasy character?
In what books can you find the characters in activity 2?

5 Match the characters from the story with their descriptions.

a)

b)

c)

d)

1 ☐ Hi! My name's Sarah. I've got red hair and I'm wearing a stripey jumper. Everybody is sad here but I'm not. I'm happy.

2 ☐ I'm the Lord of Tears. I'm tall and thin and I always wear black. I'm very unhappy and I want everybody to be unhappy, too. I hate laughter and happiness.

3 ☐ Hello. I'm Hilda and I'm a witch. But don't worry! I'm a good witch. I've got red hair. I'm wearing colourful clothes. And I've got a broom.

4 ☐ Hi, I'm Ben. I'm Sarah's best friend. I've got dark brown hair and I'm wearing a red T-shirt. I love playing my flute.

6 Look at the pictures in the book and guess the answers to the questions.

a) Who is the villain of the story?
b) What is the problem?
c) What must Sarah and Ben do to solve the problem?

"Mum," Sarah said to her mother. "Why does everybody look so sad? You and dad never smile. And when Ben and I laugh about something at school, Mr Hewitt gets angry and tells us to stop. Ben says that Mr Hewitt is grumpy●. That's why he never laughs or smiles. But what about you and dad? Why do you never smile?"

Mrs Kent sighed●. Why was Sarah always so happy and cheerful●? She said: "Maybe there is nothing to smile about. Your father and I work very hard. We have no time for silly laughter●. And why should Mr Hewitt smile? With thirty kids like you in class who talk all the time?"

Now Sarah sighed, too. She went to see her dad. "Dad," she said. "Why are you always so sad?"
"I'm not sad, I'm just tired," he said.
"But you never smile!"
"What is there to smile about?" he asked her.
And again Sarah sighed. Now she was starting to feel sad, too. "I'll go and see Ben, he'll cheer me up●," she thought. Ben was her best friend. And he always made her smile.

Glossary

- **cheer me up:** make me happy
- **cheerful:** happy
- **grumpy:** cross and irritable
- **laughter:** laughing
- **sighed:** breathed out loudly because she was sad or cross

The next morning Sarah was walking to school when she saw Ben. "Ben," she shouted. "I had a really strange dream last night."

"Me too," said Ben. "But tell me your dream first."

"Well," said Sarah, "it was a bit° scary°. There was a horrible man. He was dressed in black, and his head was like a skull°. And he had huge empty eyes."

"And big black tears were running out of his eyes and down his skull," Ben added.

"And the skull was – hey..." Sarah shouted. "How do you know that? How do you know what happened in my dream?"

"Because I had the same dream," said Ben. "Then the man said: 'I am the Lord of Tears, and soon I will be the master of the world. Soon there will be no more laughter and no more smiles. Soon there will only be tears.' And then I woke up."

"I woke up when he said that, too," said Sarah.

"But I also had another dream," said Ben.

"And in that dream I heard a lovely voice. And it said:
'Go and find the Lord of Tears. And take away the Mirror of Smiles.' "

"I had that dream, too," Sarah shouted.

" 'Follow● the setting● sun. Bring back● laughter and fun!' "

"The dream told us to go together and find the Lord of Tears," Ben said.

"Yes, let's leave this evening, when the sun is setting," said Sarah.

- **bring back:** make return
- **follow:** go after

● **setting:** (here) that is going down (in the evening)

11

Sarah and Ben packed● some food, a warm jumper each and their flutes● to play along the way. They walked and walked towards the setting sun. The sun went down and they walked on.

"I'm cold and hungry and I don't like this place," said Ben.

"Let's stop and have something to eat," said Sarah. "And then I'll play you a tune● on my flute to cheer you up."

A little while later Sarah was playing her flute and Ben looked happy.

"Hey," he said. "Did you hear that?"

Sarah stopped playing. "Hear what?" she asked.

"Someone is humming●. But I can't see anyone. Keep playing and listen."

And sure enough they could hear someone humming.

"Can you see who it is?" Ben asked Sarah.

"Hey, I'm up here. Look up, you two!"

The children looked up and saw a woman on a broom●, flying over their heads.

"Hi," she said, "nice music. Oh, I'm Hilda, by the way."

"Are you a witch?" asked Ben.

"Of course I'm a witch. Did you think I was a broom saleswoman?"

"Oh no, a witch!" said Sarah. She was frightened now.

"Don't worry, I'm a good witch," explained Hilda.

"Maybe you can help us then," said Sarah.

"We are looking for the Lord of Tears."

Glossary

- **broom:** brush witches use to fly on (see illustration)
- **flutes:** long musical instruments (see illustration)
- **humming:** making a 'hum' sound to music
- **packed:** put in a bag
- **tune:** song

12

Oops! Hilda nearly fell off her broom. She floated° down slowly and landed° in front of Sarah. "The Lord of Tears is very dangerous°. All the witches are afraid of him."

"Do you know where we can find him?" the two children asked.

"He lives behind the Mountain of Misery°."

"Can you show us the way?"

"Hop on° my broom. I'll have to ask the other witches what they think."

And they flew off through the night air.

After a while they landed in a moonlit° valley. Hilda went to talk to the other witches. Eventually° an old grey-haired woman in black clothes came over to them.

"I'm Wilhelmina, the head witch," she said. "So you want to see the Lord of Tears..."

"Yes, because we..." started Sarah.

Wilhelmina held up her hand. "Ssh, we don't want to know why."

"Can you help us find him?" Ben asked.

"Yes, we can show you the way to the Mountain of Misery. But we cannot take you to the Lord of Tears. But first we want something from you."

"What do you want?" asked Ben. "We haven't got anything."

"Oh yes, you have," replied Wilhelmina. "You've got music. We never hear music because the Lord of Tears doesn't like it."

"Okay!" said Sarah and Ben together. And they took out their flutes and played some music for the witches.

Glossary

- **dangerous:** that can hurt or damage you
- **eventually:** after some time
- **floated:** moved slowly through the air
- **hop on:** (here) get on
- **landed:** came to the ground
- **misery:** great unhappiness
- **moonlit:** that the moon lights

14

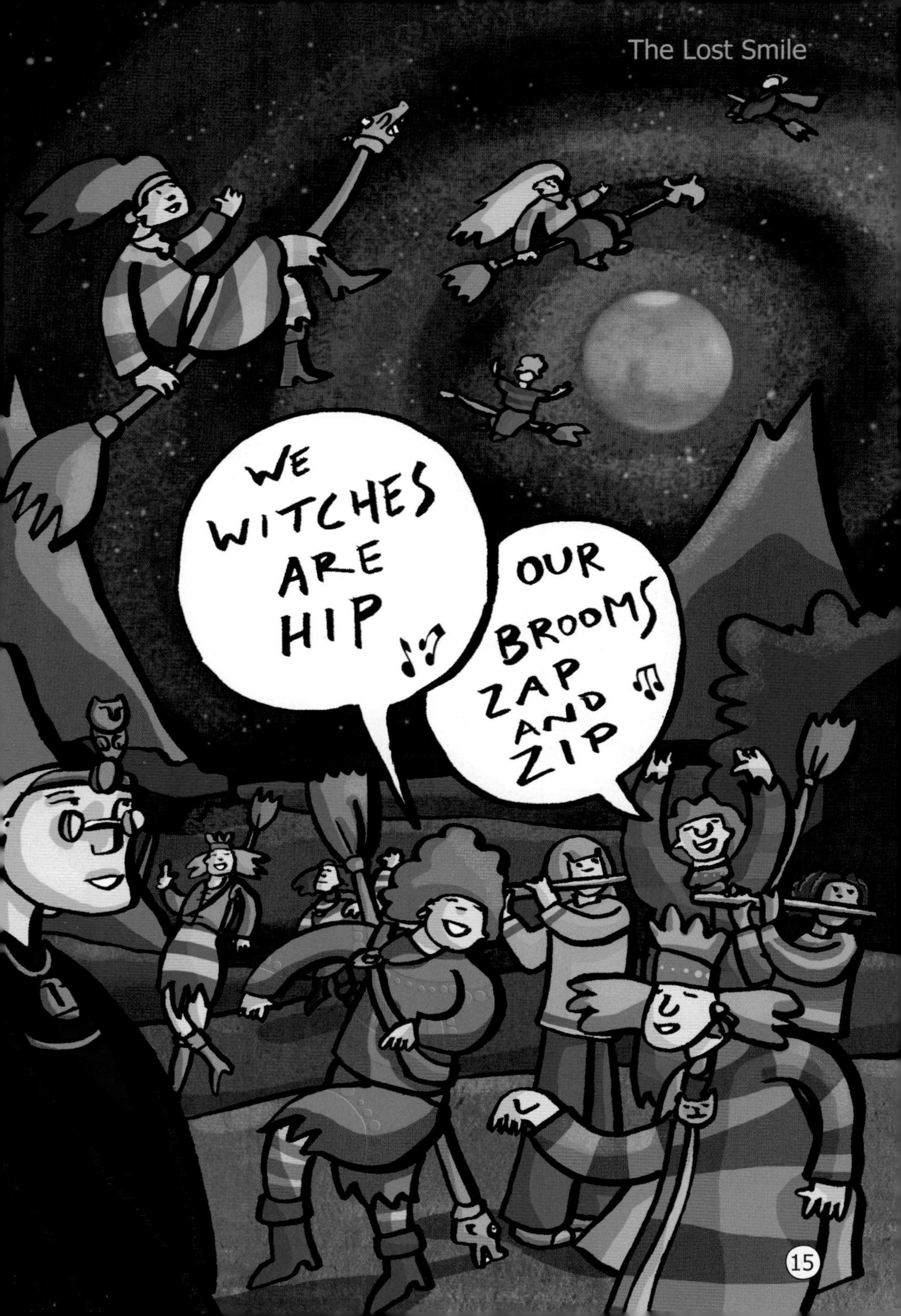
WE WITCHES ARE HIP
OUR BROOMS ZAP AND ZIP

The next morning Hilda took them to the other side of the Mountain of Misery on her broom.

They flew for ages before they landed near a little river. The grass was green, birds were singing and there were flowers everywhere. Hilda gave them each a small black stone. "This will keep you safe," she said. And she flew off again.

"This is a nice place," said Sarah, surprised. "Look at all the lovely flowers."

Ben went over to a flower and smelt it. Suddenly water ran out of the centre and down the petals.

"Ha! Ha! Ha!" The children could hear someone laughing but when they looked round there was no one there.

Suddenly Ben shouted: "Ouch! What was that? It hurt."

Glossary

- **for ages:** for a long time
- **keep you safe:** stop you from being hurt
- **ouch!:** what you shout when you are hurt or sore

16

He bent down to rub his leg and his flute fell out of his bag. Just then two little creatures° ran over and lifted his flute and started running towards some bushes.

"Hey, that's mine!" he shouted as the creatures dropped° the flute and ran off.

"Come back! Who are you?" he shouted. But there was no answer.

"Let's play some music," Sarah suggested, "maybe they'll come back."

So they sat down and played and the two little creatures came back.

"Who are you?" Sarah asked.

"We're Bill and Jill. We're goblins and we love music. Who are you? And what are you doing here?"

° **creatures:** living things   ° **dropped:** let fall

"We're Sarah and Ben. And we're on our way to find the Lord of Tears."

"The Lord of Tears?" Bill and Jill said under their breath●.

"Do you know where he lives?" asked Sarah.

"No, not really," said Bill.

"Across the Sea of Sadness," continued Jill.

"Can you show us the way●?"

"Bill can," said Jill.

"Jill can," said Bill.

"Follow us, maybe Will can," Bill and Jill said together and walked off towards the bushes. The children smiled and followed them.

A few minutes later they saw another goblin with a big bright● yellow hat.

"Hello, I'm Will," he said. "Are you sure you want to meet the Lord of Tears?"

"Yes," the children answered. "Will you help us?"

"Will I, Will, help you? Maybe, maybe not."

Sarah was getting impatient. "Will you, Will – or won't you, Will?"

"Well," Will said, "well, well, well. Will I? Yes, I will. But first you must play some music for us. The Lord of Tears has taken all our instruments."

"Sure, Will. We'll play for you."

And Ben and Sarah sat down and played some music for the goblins.

Glossary

● **bright:** (here) strong colour, full of light
● **show us the way:** tell us the correct road

● **under their breath:** in very low voices

That evening Bill and Jill took the children to the Sea of Sadness. There they gave them a boat. "Sail● west for two hours," they said. Sarah and Ben sailed west towards the setting sun. And two hours later they stopped at the shore●. All they could see were very big rocks.

"Where do we go now?" asked Ben. "I can only see rocks. There is no way out of here."

"Don't be so silly!" said a grumpy voice. "Can't you see the door?"

"Hey, who are you? Where are you?" Sarah shouted. "I can't see you, and I can't see a door!"

"I'm over here," the voice said impatiently●. And they looked in the direction of the voice and saw a dwarf with a white beard and a red cap.

"I'm Tim, the watch● dwarf. Who are you?" he said crossly. "And what are you doing in our kingdom●?"

Glossary

- **impatiently:** in a way that shows he doesn't want to wait
- **kingdom:** place where a king lives with his people
- **sail:** go in a boat
- **shore:** land beside a sea or lake
- **watch:** (here) who watches

"I'm Sarah, and this is Ben," said Sarah. "The goblins showed us the way here."

"Those pesky° goblins," Tim muttered°. "All play and no work. Not like us dwarves..."

"Sorry," said Sarah, "can we ask you something?"

"What? What?" Tim shouted. "I was talking, young lady. Don't interrupt° me." He looked at her angrily, but then he said: "Oh, alright, what do you want to know?"

"Can you tell us the way to the Lord of Tears?"

"The Lord of Tears? But we are afraid of him!"

"Please help us!"

"I'll have to talk to the other dwarves. Come, follow me," he said as he opened a door in the rock.

- **interrupt:** talk when someone else is talking
- **muttered:** said in a low voice that is difficult to understand
- **pesky:** annoying

21

The children crawled° though the open door. Now they were in a large room full of dwarves.

The children waited while Tim talked to the others. After a while one of the dwarves came over to them. "I'm Tom and I'm the head dwarf," he said. "I believe you want to meet the Lord of Tears."

"Yes," the children said. "Can you help us?"

"The Lord of Tears lives in the Fortress° of Fear°. You need to climb up a path in the rocks. But we never go there. We're afraid of him."

"Please," Sarah said, "it is very important. We must see the Lord of Tears."

"Then you must give us something," said Tom. "Have you got any gold or silver?"

"No, we haven't," Sarah and Ben said, "but we can give you some music."

"Music? We love music. Yes, that will do°!"

So Sarah and Ben played their flutes for the dwarves. Then they followed Tim up the path to the Fortress of Fear.

Soon they were at a dark stone fortress. There was an old wooden door. Sarah pushed it and it creaked° open.

Glossary

- **crawled:** went on their hands and knees
- **creaked:** made a high squeaky noise
- **fear:** when you are afraid
- **fortress:** protected castle that is difficult to enter
- **that will do:** that will be enough

"Good luck!" said Tim as the children went in. It was dark inside and very cold. They looked at each other and shivered●. There was water running down the walls and the children could hear someone crying. They walked towards the sound and soon they found the Lord of Tears. He was dressed in black and his head was like a skull and he was crying. The floor was wet with tears.

"Soon there will be only tears in the world," the Lord of Tears whispered●, "and I will be everywhere." The children looked at the water around them. It was rising● quickly. "Let's play our flutes," said Sarah. "Maybe music will stop him." And they took out their flutes and started playing. First the tears stopped and then the Lord of Tears fell asleep.

● **rising:** getting higher
● **shivered:** shook/trembled all over
  because they were cold and afraid

● **whispered:** said in a low voice

Behind the Lord of Tears' chair they saw a mirror. Ben looked into it. He saw his smiling face. "Why are you smiling?" Sarah asked. "I'm not smiling," he said, "the face in the mirror is smiling."

"This must be the Mirror of Smiles," said Sarah.

Suddenly the Lord of Tears was moving again. Sarah took the mirror and held it in front of the Lord's face. When he opened his eyes he looked straight into the mirror. In it the skull was smiling a terrible smile. Suddenly the children could hear empty laughter coming from the skull. The Lord of Tears laughed and laughed until his skull broke into a thousand pieces.

The next day Sarah woke up in her own bed at home. She went downstairs, where her mum was making breakfast.

"Hello, love," her mum said with a smile.

"Morning, Sarah," said her dad. "Hey, listen to this joke..."

Sarah looked at her parents in surprise. "You're both smiling," she said to them.

"Of course we're smiling, Sarah. Why wouldn't we?" said her dad.

Sarah met Ben on the way to school. "You'll never believe what happened at home this morning," she said.

"You parents were happy," said Ben.

"How did you know?" asked Sarah.

"Mine were too. They were smiling and joking."

"Then was it all a dream?" asked Sarah.

"I don't think so," said Ben. "Look what I found in my pocket this morning." And he showed her the black stone that Hilda had given them.

Mr Hewitt was waiting for them in class. "You're late," he said in a cross voice.
"Sir," Sarah said, "can we tell you a story?"
"What?" Mr Hewitt said, "it's not story time." But then he said: "Alright!" And the children told their story.
"Great story!" all the other kids shouted.
"I don't believe any of it," said Mr Hewitt. "But it was a good story." And slowly he started smiling.

After Reading

1 Complete the sentences with the correct names.

| Tim   Hilda   Ben and Sarah (x2)   The Lord of Tears   Bill and Jill (x2) |

    a) .... had a really strange dream.

    b) .... have to take the Mirror of Smiles.

    c) .... took Ben and Sarah on her broom to see the head witch.

    d) .... took Ben's flute.

    e) .... gave Ben and Sarah their boat to sail across the Sea of Sadness.

    f) .... took them to the Fortress of Fear.

    g) .... laughed until his skull broke.

2 Complete the sentences about the Lord of Tears with the adjectives below.

| horrible   empty   frightened   dark   dangerous |

    a) Sarah and Ben dreamt about a .... man. His name was the Lord of Tears.

    b) The Lord of the Tears was very ....

    c) He lived in a .... stone fortress.

    d) He had huge .... eyes.

    e) Everybody was .... of the Lord of Tears.

3 Now make sentences about the story with the adjectives and nouns below.

Example: *Sarah's father is very tired because he works hard.*

Adjectives	good	tired	grumpy	pesky	lovely
Nouns	father	music	goblins	witch	voice

4 Read Sarah and Ben's account of their dreams and complete the sentences with the correct tenses of the verbs below.

The First Dream

be (x4)	wear	have	cry	say (x2)

I (a) .... a really strange dream last night. There (b) .... a horrible man. He (c) .... black and he (d) .... He (e) .... that his name (f) .... the Lord of Tears. He (g) .... , "Soon there (h) .... no more laughter or smiles. There (i) .... only tears."

The Second Dream

go	bring back	hear	follow	take away

In the second dream, I (a) .... a lovely voice. It said, "(b) .... together and find the Lord of Tears and then (c) .... the Mirror of Smiles." It also said, "(d) .... the setting sun and (e) .... laughter and fun.

5 In pairs, ask and answer questions about dreams.

Do you remember your dreams?
Do you have bad dreams (nightmares)?
Tell your partner about a nightmare you had.

After Reading

Harry Potter

1 **Read and complete the fact files for the fantasy characters in the Harry Potter books by J. K. Rowling.**

Hagrid

Rubeus Hagrid's mother was a giant and his father was human so he is half human and half giant. He is very tall. He is twice as tall as a man – he is about 3.5 m tall. He has got very thick untidy hair and a big beard.

He loves magical creatures and he has got a lot of very strange and dangerous pets. He is very kind and he always helps Harry and his friends.

Name: ....

Type: Half human/half giant

Description: ....

Personality: Kind

Likes: ....

Dobby

Dobby is a house-elf in the Harry Potter series. House-elves are very small like goblins and dwarves. They have got very thin arms and legs and large heads and eyes. They have pointed ears like bats and high, squeaky voices. They are usually very obedient and they are servants to wizards. Dobby dislikes his masters, the Malfoys, and wants to be free.

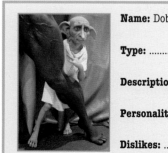

Name: Dobby

Type: ....

Description: ....

Personality: ....

Dislikes: ....

2 Create your own fantasy character. Write a fact file for it.

Is it a giant, a witch, a wizard, a goblin or a dwarf?
Is it good or evil?
What does it look like?

3 Everybody in the story is frightened of the Lord of Tears. What are these people frightened of? Listen and match the pictures.

Jane

Michael

Daniel

Rosalind

| A | B | C | D |

4 Listen again and check your answers. Then answer the questions.

a) What does Jane do when she sees a spider?
b) What could Michael never do?
c) How long was Daniel stuck in the lift for?
d) What does Rosalind do when she is in the house alone?

5 What things are people frightened of? In pairs, make a list. Then do a class survey. Ask ten people in the class what they are frightened of.

Are you frightened of spiders?

Yes, I'm terrified of them!

After Reading

1 Look at the pictures and complete the names of the places and things in the story.

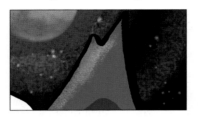

a) The .... Misery

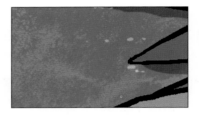

b) The .... of Sadness

c) The .... of Fear

d) The .... of Smiles

2 Now complete the text about their journey to find the Lord of Tears. Use the past simple of the verbs below and complete the names with the words in Exercise 1.

crawl	land	follow	fly	sail	find

Ben and Sarah **(a)** .... on Hilda's broom to the other side of the .... of Misery. They **(b)** .... near a little river in a moonlit valley. Then the goblins gave them their boat and they **(c)** .... across the .... of Sadness. When they stopped, they saw some big rocks. A dwarf opened a door in the rock and Ben and Sarah **(d)** .... in. Then they **(e)** .... Tim up the path to the .... of Fear. They walked into the fortress and they **(f)** .... the .... of Smiles.

3 What makes the characters in the story happy or sad? Complete the sentences with the words below.

| everything | music | Sarah and Ben's story | Ben |

a) .... always makes Sarah smile.

b) .... makes Mr Hewitt smile.

c) .... makes the Lord of Tears cry.

d) .... makes the goblins, dwarves and witches happy.

4 What makes you happy and sad, laugh or cry? Write sentences with the phrases below.

listening to a favourite CD   hearing a joke   watching the news on TV

going on holiday   being with my friends   watching a comedy film

watching a sad film   getting good grades   getting lots of homework

5 In pairs, ask and answer the questions below. Use the things in Exercise 4 or add new things.

What makes you laugh?

What makes you sad?

What makes you cry?

What makes you happy?

31

After Reading

PUZZLE

1 Can you remember these words? Read the clues and complete the puzzle with words from the story.

a) Tim, the .... takes Sarah and Ben to the Fortress of Fear.
b) In the dream, big black .... run out of the horrible man's eyes.
c) Sarah says that her teacher is ....
d) Nobody .... or smiles.
e) .... is another word for frightening.
f) Ben and Sarah .... the setting sun.
g) Ben and Sarah play the .... and make people happy.
h) Everyone is .... at the end of the story.
i) The faces in the .... always smile.
j) The Lord of Tears' skull broke into a .... pieces.

2 The letters in the green boxes spell the name of a teacher at Hogwarts in the Harry Potter series.

His name is _ _ _ _ _   _ _ _ _ _